$100,000 eBay Business

Make Insane Profits Selling on eBay & Amazon

Introduction

Thank you for purchasing this book. Whether you are new to eBay, or have been selling for a while there should be plenty of information to help you save time, sell more product, and make more money.

In my opinion, eBay is the best opportunity for the everyday person to start a business, or to make a few extra dollars on the side.

In most cases new sellers can start selling on eBay with no out of pocket expenses. All you need to do is set up an eBay and PayPal account (both are free), and start listing items you already have. When you run out of product there are plenty of simple sourcing methods available—yard sales, garage sales, estate sales, and selling for friends to name a few.

This book is short, and to the point.

Its purpose is to help you start selling on eBay as soon as possible. I have included a bonus in this print edition—the full text of my book eBay 30 Day Challenge.

Good luck, and great selling.

Table of Contents

$10,000 a Month Selling on eBay and Amazon!

Sounds impossible, doesn't it? I'm here to tell you, I've done it—and, so have thousands of other sellers.

You can too!

It's just a matter of getting started.

I have new sellers ask me every day, "What's the secret to selling on eBay?" or "What's the best way to get started selling on Amazon?"

Here's what I tell, them, and what I'm going to tell you.

"Get started.

"List your first item today. Don't worry about what you don't know, or what you think you have to know.

"Just do it!"

....

It really is that simple.

I can tell you everything I know about selling on eBay. I can tell you what products to sell. I can tell you how much to charge, and what type of listing template to use. I can tell you the best time to start and end your listings, and how to ship your items, and on—and on.

But, there's one thing I can't do.

I can't make you get started.

Think about that for a moment. Every day hundreds of people buy guides just like this one. They read them from cover to cover. Many of them underline important passages, and scribble notes in the margins, or on a notepad.

They plan what they're going to do; what they're going to sell; and how much money they're going to make.

And, then...they begin to doubt themselves. They ask themselves questions—like what if it doesn't work? What if I list my items wrong? What if my items don't sell? What'll I tell my friends if I fail?

Does any of this sound familiar?

What I'm trying to help you understand here is simple.

We're all plagued by self-doubt. Everybody questions things when they're first getting started with something new. What you've got to do if you want to become successful is to overcome these doubts.

It's like learning to walk.

You put one foot in front of the other and keep moving. If you fall down, you dust yourself off, and keep moving.

Selling online is similar to learning to walk.

You try one product or one listing. If your item doesn't sell, you find another one, and try again. If your item sells, you tweak your description or product, so you can sell even more.

If you don't learn anything else from reading this book, keep this one bit of information in the back of your mind.

Success is all about getting started.

About me

Hey there, Braun Schweiger here. I've been selling on eBay for over ten years now.

My typical work week is forty to fifty hours, Monday through Saturday, and maybe another hour on Sunday checking everything and answering emails. Most weeks I make $1200 to $1500. Some weeks I make double that. It depends on what items I have listed for sale that week.

My schedule goes something like this. I visit garage sales, estate sales, and auctions on Thursday, Friday, and Saturday. Saturday afternoon I clean everything up real good, and get it ready to photograph. Monday, Tuesday, and Wednesday I photograph and list my items.

I mail items daily Monday through Friday to meet eBay's Top Rated Seller requirements.

I've got the eBay app on my cell phone. It's set to send out notifications whenever I receive a question or sell something so I can run my business on the go. If I'm on the line about buying something—I check what it's selling for on eBay or Amazon, and make a buying decision based on real numbers—not some price I hope to get for it.

I know other sellers who hit the road for several weeks at a time like the American Pickers. They check out every estate sale and auction within a hundred miles, or five hundred miles. Most of the people who do this have a partner back home who does the actual listing, packaging, and shipping.

Several of the couples I know who do this are pulling down over $100,000 a year selling on eBay and Amazon. It's just a matter of scaling up once you get the process down.

Why you should sell on eBay & Amazon

eBay and Amazon are two of the largest ecommerce websites in the world. Together they account for over $150 billion dollars in sales every year. They have nearly 400 million registered users.

And, the best part is—they let you tap into their user base to sell your products and services.

For the average person wanting to start an online business eBay and Amazon are the easiest ways to get started. Just list your item on their website, and they will make it available to more than 400 million ready buyers. You don't have to do anything else. There's no SEO, no blogging, or costly PPC ads on Google or Facebook.

All you have to do is list your item on eBay or Amazon and you're in business.

············

If you're new to online selling—eBay and Amazon are a great way to cut your teeth in e-commerce.

Of the two sites, Amazon makes getting started the easiest. I liken it to hitch hiking on someone else's business. All you do is look for a listing similar to what you want to sell, and select the <sell on Amazon> button next to where it says "Have one to sell?" After that you follow the prompts—add your item condition, asking price, and wal-la, your item is for sale on Amazon.

It really is that simple.

Of course, not every item you run across is going to be available for sale on Amazon. Sometimes you stumble across a new or unique item no one has listed for sale yet. Not a problem. Amazon has a tool that lets you create a new listing page for it. We'll talk more about using it later in this guide.

Amazon also has a few restrictions on products you can sell, especially around Christmas and other big holidays. They don't want the little guys selling against them or their big merchants in these product lines. It's just one of those things you need to deal with. Most times when I bump into one of these categories Amazon shows me that my listing has been blocked. Translation: it's not being shown to visitors on the Amazon website. It's still there, but only Amazon and I can see it.

....

eBay offers a similar feature. Under the pictures at top of the item listing page you'll see the words, "Have one to sell?" Next to that you'll see some blue text that says <Sell now>. Select that and it will bring up an item description page pre-populated with many of the item details you need to list the item.

It's not quite as simple to use as Amazon's piggybacking feature, but with a few tweaks you can produce a great looking listing page. eBay requires you to add at least one picture of the product you are trying to sell. You can also change the description a bit to better fit what your selling, maybe talk about the color, any accessories you are including, and add a little detail describing any of the rough spots. Doing this helps potential buyers get a better feel for the item you're selling.

And, just like Amazon, eBay lets you add new listing pages from scratch when you have an item that is unique to the website. We'll get more into that in another chapter. For now, just keep in mind eBay and Amazon give you lots of flexibility in how you list and sell your items. The exact listing method you decide to use should be dictated by the item you are selling, the venue you choose to list it on, and what your individual sales goals are.

Which site should you sell on?

Often times, your products will sell equally well on eBay or Amazon. Other times, one site is better suited to what you are selling.

How do you decide which site is the best for what you are selling?

Generally speaking, eBay is better suited for selling unique, higher priced items, or items you are unsure about the value of. If you've got multiples of an item, eBay's auction feature allows you to experiment and test the waters. Auctions also give you a chance to get a higher price for items you are unsure of the value of, or items that have no set pricing. If you're nervous about not getting the right price for the item you're selling, you can set a reserve price. If your item doesn't reach the reserve price, it doesn't sell.

Use Amazon to list everyday items—books, textbooks, clothes, shoes, cell phones, and other electronics. Just about anything that is a consistent seller, and sells within a set price range is the perfect item for selling on Amazon.

Amazon's fees are similar to what eBay charges. Final value fees are slightly higher, but they include payment processing fees. (On eBay, you have to make an extra payout to PayPal for credit card processing.) Another great thing about Amazon is they don't charge listing fees. Amazon only gets paid if your item sells.

Amazon also makes it easier to determine how quickly your items should sell. Amazon ranks every item based upon how well it sells. Let's look at books as an example. There are millions of books listed for sale on Amazon. Each one has a product ranking from one to blah-blah million. The lower the ranking of the book, the better the sales of the book are. Books ranked under 100 are super-fast sellers; books ranked under 10,000 are consistently good sellers; and books ranked under 50,000 are still selling several copies per week.

Once you're familiar with Amazon's ranking system, it makes it easier to pick consistent winners.

To discover the best sellers on eBay takes a little more work. By employing eBay's advanced search feature you can get a good idea how many of each item sold recently, and how much they sold for. By consistently using this information to source product you can pick better selling merchandise to list.

What Should I Sell

The first question most new sellers have is, "What should I sell?"

The simple answer is, "Whatever strikes your fancy."

As long as it's legal to sell, and doesn't violate either company's terms of service (TOS), feel free to list it and sell it. Some of the items you can't sell on eBay are guns, body parts (livers, eye balls, hearts, kidneys, and such), designer knockoffs and counterfeits, and Native American art and artifacts produced after a certain date. Amazon is a little fussier, because they reserve certain categories and items just for themselves and their favorite sellers. The items individual sellers can offer also vary by season. You'll have to read the TOS for more information on that.

I can tell you Amazon just changed its rules for selling DVDs with an MSRP over $25.00. You now need prior approval from Amazon before listing these items.

....

I always recommend new sellers start out by selling items they already have. There's no sense buying scads of new stuff to sell before you're sure selling on eBay and Amazon agrees with you.

Most everybody has extra stuff lying around the house that other people might want. Here's a short list to help get your creative juices flowing about things you can sell.

- Old and unused cell phones

- Jewelry (bracelets, rings, necklaces, etc.)

- Books (anything out of print, reference books, college textbooks. Generally, nonfiction sells better than fiction. Newer fiction and recently published paperbacks are a tough sell because there are so many of them available.)

- Clothes (designer clothes are great sellers, children's name brand clothes, plus size clothes for men and women, jeans, and slightly worn shoes)

- Kitchen gadgets (this category covers any of those goodies you see on late night TV shows and infomercials—George Foreman grills, Nu Wave ovens, or anything by Ronco or Popeil. Most people are suckers for gadgets they've seen on TV, especially if the price is right.)

- Collectibles (stamps, coins, baseball cards, Hummel figurines—all of these sell very well. Items sold originally as collectibles, such as anything by Franklin Mint, don't sell well. There are too many of them available, and too few buyers.)

- Toys (Hot toys sell well, especially around the holidays. Vintage toys are great sellers—Easy Bake

Oven, Rock Em Sock Em Robots, Barbie, and G I Joe. So be sure to check the attic and see if mom and dad stashed any of your old toys away.)

- Used computers / software (Used computers, tablets, and laptops are quick sellers. Broken and non-working electronics usually sell well. Repair shops and tinkerers harvest them for re-useable parts. Software can be a nightmare to resell. Some companies, like Intuit don't make it easy to transfer licenses, so their programs are worthless to second hand buyers. Other manufacturers like Microsoft limit the number of times their software can be used, so new purchasers might find themselves left out in the cold.

- Car parts (Used car parts are a big business and sell well online. If you've got some old parts lying around the garage, list them on eBay. If you're handy and have an old junker ready for the scrap yard, consider piecing it out on eBay instead. You should be able to pull down some good money.)

- Movies / music (Old DVDs, CDs, and VHS tapes sell well online, particularly if they're limited editions or hard to find. Blank cassettes and VHS tapes are good sellers, too.)

Hopefully that gives you a good idea of some easy to find items you can sell on eBay and Amazon. Once you start looking you should be able to locate dozens of other sellable items.

Make it a point to practice selling these items first.

This lets you do two things. One—get comfortable selling online, and two—make sure this business is right for you.

Not everyone is cut out for online selling. It's more work than most people think. It eats up a lot of time, there's a long learning curve (if you want to do things right), and there are lots of ups and downs—financially. Even eBay Power Sellers have weeks and months when sales—and income dry up or disappear.

It happens.

If you're not prepared for it, it can cause real hardship, or drive you out of the business.

Start Selling on eBay

Pretty near every writer begins their spiel about selling on eBay by talking about what to sell or how to sell, but they're all missing the most important element to continued success selling on eBay—building a strong reputation. If you don't have awesome feedback it's going to be tough to grow your sales.

If you're unfamiliar with buying and selling on eBay, buyers and sellers can rate each other based on a five star rating system. The system is somewhat skewed towards buyers because if they are unhappy, they can leave negative feedback for the seller. Sellers can no longer leave negative feedback for buyers.

It's this feedback rating buyers look at to determine whether it's safe to purchase an item from a particular seller. Generally speaking if two sellers are offering the same item at a similar price, buyers will make their purchase from the seller who has better feedback. It just makes sense to spend your money with someone who has a good reputation.

As a result, your number one goal is to ensure that customers are delighted with their purchases, and leave you great feedback.

Sounds easy, doesn't it?

Let's look at a couple examples that can cause the buyer to leave negative feedback.

- When customers make a purchase, eBay shows buyers an estimated delivery time. Top rated sellers generally ship their items within 24 hours, which means they're doing their part to ensure the item is delivered on time. Many times—the post office delivers packages outside of eBay's estimated delivery time. When this happens disgruntled buyers sometimes leave sellers negative feedback, even though the late delivery has nothing to do with them.

- Sometimes purchasers suffer from buyer's remorse and change their mind before the seller ships the item. Before September 20th, 2014 that wasn't a big problem. The seller could send in a request to cancel the sale, and when the buyer accepted it everything was ok. The reality today with eBay grading sellers on the defect system means when a buyer changes their mind they're really putting the seller on the spot. The seller is forced to choose between offering good customer service and canceling the sale, or telling the customer "sorry— you're going to have to contact eBay to do that." The reason is when the buyer makes the request to cancel, the seller isn't charged with a defect. But, wait—there's a massive "Catch 22" lurking here. If the seller waits for the cancellation to go through eBay, the odds are he's going to be late with his agreed upon shipping time. That's a seller defect.

Too many of them and you can be thrown off of eBay.

- Here's a similar situation. Many times customers make a purchase and then ask the seller to hold off on mailing the item until they return from vacation, or until it's closer to the recipient's birthday. Good customer service says you should hold the item for the specified time period, but if you do—eBay looks at it as a seller defect.

These are some of the situations you're going to face trying to offer good customer service while at the same time trying to maintain a low defect rate with eBay. I can't tell you how to deal with these issues. It's something you're going to have to work out on a case-by-case basis.

That's a quick overview of customer service.

....

Selling on eBay is all about creating great product listings that get customers excited about what you're selling.

When you create your listing you need to –

1. Create a title loaded with keywords

eBay gives you 88 characters to describe what you're selling. Make them count.

Here's a secret a lot of sellers don't know or understand. Your title contains the search terms for what you're selling. It's how buyers find what you're selling amongst the millions of other things for sale on eBay.

Don't waste words. Make every keyword you include in your title count. The easiest way to do this is to think about how you'd search for that item. What words would you use? What are the most important things you're looking for? Some of the obvious choices are—manufacturer, model number, color, condition—new, used, and refurbished, free shipping, and easy returns.

2. Take large well lit photos

Selling online is all about the pictures. Every day the internet is becoming more of a visual experience. Think about social media. The most shared items today are short videos, cat pictures, pictures of adults and children acting stupid, and those cutesy illustrations with quotes attached to them.

What does that mean for online sellers?

You need to include large clear pictures in all of your listings. They need to show the item you're selling from a number of different angles. If the item you're selling has any damage you need to include close up pictures of the affected areas.

Your pictures should be so clear your customer feels they can reach out and touch what you're selling. A cover designer on Fiverr explained this better than I ever could. She said the chocolate shown on her covers is so realistic you'll want to lick it.

Make all of your pictures that good, and you'll find yourself making more sales for more money than ever before.

Here's another tip. Find a way to include video in your listings. There's something about videos that compels people to watch them.

3. Write a benefit driven description

The majority of sellers recite all of these droll facts about what they're selling. "I have a yellow taxi cab from 1964. It has an AM radio, bald tires, a spare tire, and oh yeah—it only runs when you can get a few friends together to give it a push." Slightly humorous, but dull. It doesn't contain anything that compels you to buy the yellow taxi.

You need to create listings that mimic the way people read on the internet. Most people read the headlines, and then skim through the copy looking for details that interest them. if you list your key points using bullet points your customers eyes are going to move directly from the headlines to the bullet points.

Another mistake sellers make is rambling off a slew of features. Customers don't care about features. They want to know what's in it for them. Tell them the benefits.

- Your new TV comes equipped with a full featured remote so you never have to get out of your chair to change the channel or adjust the volume.

- Your new theater chairs are awesome. They have a built-in refrigerator and urination control system, so you never miss a moment of programming to grab another beer or go number one.

4. Research your item, and price it to sell.

Inexperienced sellers rush to post their listings for sale, and settle for whatever price they get. Successful online sellers research every item before they post their listing. That way they know how likely it is to sell, how much money they can reasonably expect to get for it, and what the best keywords are to include in their title and listing description.

They know that the more time and research they put into selling an item the more money they're going to make.

5. Manage buyer expectations

This means you need to describe your item—warts and all.

Making a successful sale online or in person is all about managing buyer expectations. Your listing needs to get buyers excited about what you're selling. You need to make them visualize your item, and picture how much fun they're going to have using it. But, before you go in for the kill, you need to make them pull back for a moment. List any defects or blemishes your item has. If you're selling a cell phone, be sure to tell potential buyers which carriers it is and is not compatible with.

Many sellers are afraid to mention problems or defects, because they think it will kill the sale. A lot of times it does just the opposite. When you take time out to explain defects and any potential problems they may encounter buyers are more likely to feel they can trust you.

Start Selling on Amazon

As I said earlier, selling on Amazon is easier than selling on eBay.

To list an item for sale on Amazon just search for an item similar to the one you want to sell. Look the listing over to make sure it's the proper edition, variation, size, or whatever. When you're sure it's the correct item, look for the text that says "Have one to sell." Select the box next to it that says <Sell on Amazon>.

When you select <Sell on Amazon> it pulls up the listing page. Verify that it's the correct item. Select the appropriate condition, and make any condition notes in the box. Below that list the quantity available and your asking price. After you input the quantity available you're given the opportunity to upload up to six images. The final step is to select your shipping preferences. You can select one shipping method, or all of them. One thing I've discovered is most buyers go with the least expensive shipping option, but your item will sell quicker if you offer more options. Try it for yourself and see what happens.

Select continue and you will be taken to a summary page that reviews your selections, and recaps your asking price and the expected Amazon fees if your item sells. It also tells you how much money you will receive after Amazon fees, and how much your shipping credit is.

If you have more than one of each item to sell don't just list them together for the same price. Carefully examine their condition, and if one item is in better condition list it separately. Normally you can charge a higher price for an item in better condition.

A close look at the book category shows prices ranging from 99¢ to $25.00 or more depending upon the book's condition. That's why it's so important to grade your book properly. In poor to good condition it may sell for 99¢, but the next step up can increase the selling price by $3.00 to $5.00. Best advice. Grade your book as high as the condition warrants, but don't bump the grade just to make a few extra bucks. Grading items incorrectly is a sure way to get returns, or negative feedback.

....

Unless you sell one of a kind collectibles the listing method shown above is going to work for most of the items you list on Amazon.

When you have a unique item to sell that hasn't previously been listed on Amazon you can add a new page to the Amazon catalog. It takes a few more steps, but will be a breeze after you've completed a few.

Follow these steps to add a new listing page to the Amazon catalog.

1. In Amazon Seller Central go to the inventory page and select <Add a Product>.
2. Enter the name of the product you want to list, the ISBN, or UPC.
3. Select a category to list your item in.
4. From here you will be taken to the listing page.

Most listing pages have six separate sections.

- **Vital info** lets you enter the title for your item. Amazon allows you to add up to 250 characters. These are the search terms for your listing so make your keywords count. The other information you're asked for depends upon the item you're selling. Fill in as much information as possible.

- **Offer** lets you add a SKU (an identification number for the product. If you don't enter one, Amazon will select one for you.) This is also where you enter price, and the number of items you have for sale. Select the condition, add a condition note if needed, and select your shipping methods.

- **Images** is where you enter your product photos. Amazon requires photos to be 1000 pixels on the longest edge, and 500 pixels along the shortest edge. You're allowed up to eight pictures. Use as many as you need to sell your item.

- **Product description** gives you 2000 characters to describe your item. Keep it short and concise. List any accessories included with your item, and if there is damage—describe it. Unlike eBay— Amazon does not allow you to list any branding information about yourself or your business, so keep your description focused on the product you're selling.

- **Keywords** lets you add keywords and search terms to make it easier for buyers to find what you're selling. Each section has four spaces that accept up to 50 characters.

- **More details** lets you include item and package dimensions.

After you've completed all six sections select <save and finish> at the bottom and your item should be listed on Amazon within fifteen to thirty minutes.

The above categories will vary based upon what you are selling. The example I used was from the books category.

12 Tips to Grow Your Business

Here are twelve tips that will help you grow your business and make more money. Use one, or use all of them. They've helped myself and many other sellers build a more successful online business.

1. Offer amazing customer service

I said it earlier, I'm going to say it again—customer service is the most important element of selling on eBay.

Customer service begins with a great listing. Provide large clear photos of every item you sell. If the item you're selling has any damage or blemishes, take close up pictures of those areas. Give customers the information they need, and let them decide if the item is right for them or not.

The same thing goes for your description.

Make it short, easy to read, and benefit focused. Get right to the point. Identify the product, model number, maker, and any other relevant information. If it's new in the box, or new without tags, tell your buyer exactly what they're getting. If the item is damaged in any way, describe the damage, and refer the customer to your photos so they can make their own decision.

Finally, list the benefits buyers will enjoy when they purchase your item.

- This digital camera comes with a backup battery, so you can take pictures to your heart's content and never worry about running out of power.

- This heavy duty rubber case protects your iPhone whether you drop it from 1 inch or 10 feet. Stop worrying, and start enjoying your new iPhone.

Do you understand the difference? No one wants an extra battery; they want the satisfaction they get from not having to worry about their battery going dead. No one wants a heavy duty rubber iPhone case; they want to know their phone is protected from accidental damage.

When you focus on the benefits customers will receive from buying your item, you make them scream out, "Yeah! I have to have that."

And, that brings us to the final point. Keep your description short. Use plenty of white space, headlines, and bullet points.

Make it easy for buyers to find the information they're looking for.

You also have to follow up with buyers. When a potential buyer sends a request asking for more information, answer the email promptly. Use the eBay app so you know when someone asks a question while you're at work or on the go. If you can't answer the specific question right away, tell the customer you're away from your office, but will get back to them as soon as possible.

Then give them a time frame, and follow up within that time period.

When you answer a customer inquiry there are all sorts of ways to approach it. Perhaps the best is to thank the customer for contacting you, give them a little information about the item and your business, and then answer the specific question.

Let's say a customer contacts you about an iPad you're selling, and is concerned about a scratch on the screen shown in one of your pictures. Here's an example of how to respond to that customer.

"Thank you for visiting Braun's Apple-o-rama. We do our best to offer top quality used and refurbished Apple products at the best possible prices. One way we do that is by accurately describing every product we sell, and providing clear accurate photos of the item you're buying. To answer your question, I just looked at the iPad you inquired about. It's in real nice shape, and comes with a case, and charger. The scratch you're asking about is roughly ½ inch long, and runs along the surface. It does not go deep into the screen. I tested it out using Word and the internet, and am happy to report the scratch does not affect viewing at all. I hope that answers all of your questions, and keep in mind we offer a 14 day 100% satisfaction guarantee—so if you're unhappy for any reason, you're free to return the item."

What do you think?

It's friendly. It tells a little more about your business, and how you approach selling online. It answers the customer's specific question, and it goes a step further to sell the item by stressing the 14 day money back guarantee.

Try using this approach in your business emails. Your customers are going to love it.

2. Use eBay / Amazon Shipping tools

A lot of sellers still waste time hand addressing their packages and taking them to the post office.

eBay and Amazon have built in tools that make it easier to ship the items you sell, and save you time and money. By using online shipping tools you also help to ensure your customers receive their items quicker.

Here are some of the ways using these tools can help you ship more efficiently.

- eBay and Amazon shipping tools automatically transfer the customer information to your shipping label. As a result you don't have to worry about addressing mistakes.

- The shipping tools verify addresses against postal records to ensure you're shipping to a valid address. If it turns out the customer provided a bad address you can correct it before shipping your item. That saves you the cost of reshipping an item, and by verifying the address is correct, it helps your customer get their package quicker.

- When you use eBay and Amazon shipping tools you receive a discount over rates you would receive from going to the post office. In most cases tracking is free when you print your shipping labels online. That saves you a minimum of $1.05 for each item you ship.

- You can order packing supplies needed to ship items by priority and express mail, and you can schedule a home pick up so the post office comes to you, rather than waste your time taking packages to them.

More advanced sellers, or sellers who transact business on more than one ecommerce platform, may want to check out Stamps.com or Endicia. They collect all of your orders from the different platforms and let you ship from one console.

3. Research everything

You never know. That item you bought for a dollar might be worth $500, or $5,000. Before you start it at 99¢ do a little research first, so you know what you've got.

On Amazon you can tell how well an item is selling by looking at its product rank. In most cases Amazon gives a rank from 1 (being the bestselling item) to blah-blah million (being the slowest seller in that category). When you're sourcing products to sell, you want to pick items that rank under 100,000 whenever possible. This means that in most categories the products are still selling one or two items per week.

Some sellers hit book sales and clearance aisles of Wal-Mart, Target, and T J Maxx with scanners and scouting software to help select the items most likely to sell fastest for the best profit. If this sounds like something that might be of interest to you check out *Barcode Booty* by Steve Weber. It covers the topic of using scanning software in more detail.

If you're an occasional seller, download the Amazon or eBay app to your smartphone. Check what some of the items you're considering purchasing actually sell for on eBay. It will help you make more informed choices.

If you're selling on eBay there are a number of research tools available from eBay and from third party sellers. The most useful tool for sellers is eBay's advanced search tab. It lets you see how many items have recently sold, how much they sold for, the listing method used for making the sale, and the starting price and or buy-it-now price.

My advice is to conduct basic research before listing any item. You can use the information to set a price and help select keywords and description ideas.

To access the advanced search tool, scroll up to the top of the eBay page where you see the search bar. Next to it you'll see the word **advanced**. Select it, and you're ready to roll.

4. Offer refunds

No one likes to take things back. You're on eBay to make money, not give it back.

The truth is a generous refund policy will help you sell more items. Buying online is scary. No matter how many items you've bought on eBay or Amazon, you always have lingering doubts—did the seller accurately describe his item? Is that new iPhone he's selling really new in the box, or is it a refurbished model being passed off as new?

Go ahead. Admit it. You've had those same doubts when you were getting ready to make an online purchase.

Take it from someone who's offered a 100 per cent satisfaction policy for the past ten years, offering to give a refund doesn't mean customers are going to take advantage of you.

People are basically honest. As long as you accurately describe what you're selling, and grade the condition honestly, customers are going to be pleased with their purchases. The majority of refunds happen because of misunderstandings about item condition.

Your job as a seller is to help set buyer expectations so they understand what they're buying. You do this by describing any damage or problems, and by posting large clear photographs.

5. Take great photos

The old saying is, "A picture is worth a thousand words." On eBay and Amazon a picture can easily be worth a thousand dollars.

Throughout this book I've talked about the importance of taking great pictures. Pictures are the key to making more sales on eBay and Amazon. When buyers shop at a retail store they can pick items up, look them over, touch them, turn them over, and get a real feel for what they're buying. If you want to make more sales online, your pictures have to give customers that same shopping experience.

How do you do it?

The first thing you need is a good camera. The eBay app lets you post listings from your iPhone or smartphone, and that's fine for occasional sellers. If you're a professional seller, that's not going to cut it. Cell phone pictures often come out grainy and they're hard to edit.

A good digital camera with a variety of lenses will let you take the best possible pictures. Most of the new cameras make it as easy as 1 – 2 – 3. You just point, the camera, press the button, and you get a great picture.

If you're photographing a lot of small items consider purchasing a light box. You can pick one up on eBay or Amazon starting at $30.00. A light box normally comes with several floodlights, a tent-like structure to photograph your item in, a small tripod, and several different colored backdrops. The biggest advantage of using a light box is you can take close up photos of smaller items without worrying about dark backgrounds or weird looking shadows in your pictures.

If you're selling bigger items—furniture, bikes, exercise equipment, cars, etc. photograph them outside. It will give you the best possible lighting.

Best advice. Look every item you're selling over before you photograph it. If there's any kind of damage make sure you take pictures of the damage from several different angles. Next think about what you're selling. What do customers need to see to purchase the item? How many different angles do you need to photograph it from? Are there working parts that customers would want to see? If you're selling a laptop or phone, would it make sense to show it lit up and working? How about accessories? If it comes with a power cord, CDs, ear buds, or a case, you should probably have a grouped photo of them.

Use as many pictures as you need to tell your story. Keep in mind eBay requires your picture to be at least 500 pixels along the longest edge. They recommend 1600 pixels for optimal viewing when your picture is enlarged. Amazon requires pictures to be at least 1000 pixels along the largest end, and at least 500 pixels along the shortest end.

6. Develop a pricing strategy

Sellers have all sorts of pricing strategies. Some like to go for the highest price possible, others start everything at 99¢ and are happy with whatever they get. Still others shoot for the middle ground, thinking they don't need to get the highest price possible, but they'd still like a decent return on their investment.

Best advice. Determine a pricing strategy before you start selling online. Understand up front that it's okay to be the high price seller or the low price seller, as long as you know why you're at that price point.

If you sell cheap crap, or rush to list a hundred items a day without putting any thought or time into them then the best you can hope for is to get the low price. If, on the other hand, you take time out to carefully research each item, shoot amazing photographs, and write an awesome benefit driven description, you have every right to ask for—and receive a higher price.

The price your item sells for is ultimately up to you. What I suggest is to look at different items being sold on eBay and the different prices sellers are asking for them. You'll find a lot of books, clothes, whatever that people are asking a crazy amount of money for. But, you'll also see a lot of sellers who pop the same item up for sale starting at 99¢ or $9.99. The low end sellers generally have a single blurry picture, a short blah-blah description, and mixed or negative feedback. High end sellers include six to twelve well lit photos in each listing, and use the description to build value into the item and really sell it.

The choice is entirely up to you. You can nickel and dime your way to mediocre success, or you can sell fewer items and make more money.

The profit you make on eBay is all about how you approach your listing.

Amazon is an entirely different animal when it comes to pricing. Because most items are sold off of the same listing page you have to stick to a lower price to stay in the ball game. The trick to making more sales on Amazon is to grade your items properly so you can sell your item as a higher grade article.

Another secret to making money on Amazon is to steer away from the pack, and create your own items to sell. It's not hard. Bundle a collection of James Patterson books together. Instead of listing each book for sale at 99¢ individually, price your bundle at $25.00. Create Halloween or birthday party packs centered around a theme. Include piñatas, plates, napkins, party favors and bags. If you're selling electronic parts or kits include a short video or booklet that explains how to use them or hook them up. Now you're selling a complete solution rather than just a cord or a pile of parts. It makes it different enough from what other sellers are offering, so you can create your own listing page and ask for more money.

The trick is to make your item unique. That way you can create your own sales page on Amazon. When you do this competition and price are no longer a factor. You can create an amazing description, and ask for—and receive a premium price.

Whenever possible, ask yourself how you can stack the deck in your favor. It'll pay off every time.

7. Choose a niche to sell in

Anybody can sell a little bit of everything on eBay. Most Top Rated Sellers learned early on they can make more sales and charge higher prices by specializing in a niche.

Brick and mortar stores rely on repeat customers to grow their business. Online sellers are no different. Repeat customers are going to be the lifeblood of your online business.

If you're selling clothes this week, books the next week, and bathroom accessories the week after it's going to be tough to build a repeat clientele. If you specialize in one product line, you're more likely to attract repeat buyers. If someone buys something from you that they like or collect, and they see you regularly sell similar items, they're more likely to check back to see what's next. Curiosity is your best friend. It will bring many buyers back to see what you're offering next week, and the week after.

As long as you don't disappoint customers, and continue offering new and unique items in your niche, they will keep coming back for more.

The question you're probably asking yourself is, "How do I let buyers know that I offer similar items?" Both eBay and Amazon offer online stores to their sellers. Make sure you set them up, and keep them stocked with new and exciting items.

It's easier to brand yourself on eBay. Each eBay listing invites buyers to visit your eBay store, or to view your other listings. Because Amazon is a marketplace made up of many sellers for each individual item, buyers don't get that nudge to look at individual listings from a single buyer. They can visit your Amazon storefront, but to do so, they need to know how to navigate there. Most buyers don't.

Let's talk about branding on eBay for a few more moments.

eBay offers sellers numerous opportunities to brand yourself. The most obvious one is to open an eBay store. You can design a custom storefront and listing template that makes shopping with you unique. You can include your logo, tag line, and any other info you care to include about yourself or your business. The downside is doing this is expensive, and using HTML code in your listings has been found to hurt sales coming from mobile devices.

An easier and less expensive way to encourage repeat buyers is to talk about your other items in each of your listings. Remind buyers to check back regularly because you have a fluid inventory that is constantly changing and you have new items arriving every week. If you've made a special purchase you'll be listing in upcoming weeks talk it up in all of your listings. If you sell winter coats, mention visitors should check your eBay store for a great selection of gloves, scarfs, and hats. If you sell digital cameras, tell buyers to visit your store for batteries, bags, books, and lenses.

Make it fun. Make it educational. Motivate your buyers to come back and check you out week after week. It will build repeat buyers, and encourage customers to recommend you to their friends.

8. Sell international

Most new sellers avoid international sales like the plague. Many of them have heard horror stories about items lost or stolen in transit, areas that form a Bermuda Triangle like zone that suck up eBay packages, and dishonest buyers who will take you for whatever they can get.

The actual truth about international selling is quite different than most people's perception of it. The majority of international sales go smoothly with many customers in Europe receiving their packages quicker than buyers here in the United States.

Several years ago eBay instituted something called the Global Shipping Program that makes selling internationally no different than selling domestically.

The way it works is sellers opt into the Global Shipping Program when they list their item for sale. If their item sells to an international buyer, eBay provides the seller with the address of one of their shipping partners. You ship the item to eBay's U S shipping center, and your part in the transaction is completed. From that point on, eBay and Pitney Bowes are responsible for the safe delivery of your package.

It doesn't get much simpler than that.

And, in case you're still not convinced selling internationally is in your best interest, consider this—Most of the growth eBay sellers are experiencing is a direct result of international sales. Many successful sellers on eBay and Amazon draw as much as forty to fifty percent of their sales from international customers.

If you choose only one method to grow your sales, sell international.

9. Open an eBay store

If you're serious about selling on eBay, open an eBay store. Over time, it's going to save you money. These days, eBay stores come with a variety of useful features— free and discounted product listings, discounting tools, extra pages to provide additional product information, and email list building tools.

Think of an eBay store as your own little space on the internet. Back in prehistoric eBay times (the early 2000's), most items sold at auction. On a good week 40 to 50 percent of the items you listed sold. If you relisted them two or three times a few more would sell.

The mathematicians among you have probably already figured out that that still leaves roughly 40 percent of your listings unsold. That begs the question, what's a seller to do with the rest of your items? One choice was to delete them, and figure they had their day, and no one wanted them. Another choice was to pack them away in an eBay store and wait for buyers to stumble across them. In those dark days eBay didn't display store listings in search, potentials buyers had to do some extra work to ferret them out.

I took the last option, and over time I packed nearly 10,000 items away in my eBay store. The funny thing was—over time, I was selling more items from my eBay store than I was from my auction listings. If I took a week or two off from listing items, I could still make $500 or a $1000 a week.

And, that's the real beauty of an eBay store. I liken it to building an annuity. Not listing items for sale one week or listing a slew of bad items now and then won't kill your business. Your eBay store will help level out your sales and your income.

An eBay store comes with a number of seller tools that can help you ratchet up your sales.

- Markdown Manager lets you run spot sales. You can choose how long you want your sale to run, the percentage discount or dollar discount you want to offer and which items you want to include in the sale.

- Mail list manager lets you build a mailing list of customers who sign up to receive mailings from you. Each time you create a sale with Markdown Manager you can choose to have eBay send an email to your customer list.

- Custom pages allow you to create additional pages to provide more information to your potential customers. Some sellers use them to provide sizing information for clothing, other sellers use them to talk about the product they sell, or how carefully they package and ship items. How you use your custom pages is entirely up to you.

- Promotional boxes let you collect and receive information from your customers. I use mine to explain my shipping policies and prices, ask customers to sign up for my mailing list, and I have one in the sidebar to my store that introduces new customers to my business and the products I sell.

- Custom categories let you set up sections within your eBay store that make it easier for customers to find items they're searching for.

10. Build an email marketing list on and off of eBay.

Things change. Selling on eBay and Amazon may be the greatest thing going today, and you may be making all the money you want. But, tomorrow is another day.

You never know what's around the corner. There are a lot of former eBay power sellers who woke up one morning and discovered their entire $100,000 a year eBay business turned upside down.

Think it can't happen to you?

Five years ago, digital download products (eBooks) were some of the hottest sellers on eBay. Many sellers were cashing in selling hundreds of them per day. A lot of other sellers purchased them just to get quick feedback. And, then one day, eBay announced they were banning the sale of digital downloads. The new rules prohibited digital downloads and required that all eBooks had to be physically shipped to buyers on a CD or some other media. Thousands of power sellers saw their businesses destroyed overnight.

More recently, eBay has upgraded seller standards and changed the way they grade seller performance. Five star feedback isn't good enough anymore. Sellers are evaluated based upon their defect rate. One and two star ratings count as defects. So does cancelling orders because you ran out of stock or any other reason. If your defect rate is over five percent, eBay reserves the right to limit or suspend your selling privileges. The new policy went into effect in September of 2014, but depending on how many sales you make, they reach back from three to twelve months to determine if you're in compliance. To date thousands of five star sellers have been booted off of eBay for no other reason than eBay changed the way they evaluate your performance.

Amazon has been known to make similar changes. At certain times of the year, especially around Christmas only preapproved sellers are allowed to sell in certain categories. Other categories are limited to favored sellers year round. Most recently Amazon decided only a select group of sellers would be allowed to sell DVDs with an MSRP over $25.00. Many DVD retailers found themselves stuck with unsellable inventory, while at the same time having their ability to make a living limited.

That's why I say, no matter how well your online business is doing today—start building a mailing list to protect and grow your business.

....

The first thing you need to know is when you make a sale on eBay and Amazon—according to both company's TOS those customers belong to eBay and Amazon—not you, so you need to be careful how you contact them.

eBay lets you build an email list using their tools, but the email list belongs to them, and all emails must be sent through their email service.

The best way for sellers to build their email list on eBay is to include a promotional box on your eBay store page that asks sellers to join your email list. You can also suggest in your listings that sellers join your email list so they know about upcoming sales and special events. When you do this, each time you create a sale using Markdown Manager you can send an announcement to your customer list.

Building a mailing list off eBay requires a little more effort and subterfuge.

Be sure to include a thank-you note in each package you send. Let customers know if they have any problems or questions you'll be happy to help them out. If you have a website, list your URL and suggest customers visit it often as you're constantly adding new items to your inventory.

Suggest customers join your mailing list. Offer them a free gift or special discount for doing so.

When you invite customers to join your list you're going to need an email service to sign them up. Some of the more popular email services are Mail Chimp, Constant Contact, and A Weber. The reason you don't want to do it yourself is there are privacy laws in place concerning email contact and sending spam emails. These services allow customers to easily opt into and out of your email program, thus ensuring you are in compliance with government regulations.

Detailed instructions about building an email list are beyond the scope of this book. Here are a few sources you may find helpful if you decide to setup an email list for your online business.

- Email Marketing Blueprint by Steve Scott

- *Email Marketing That Doesn't Suck* by Michael Clark, Stever Ure, and Desy Simmons

- Email marketing for Dummies by Arnold

11. Get a Face Lift

Update your eBay store.

I'm a meat and potatoes kind of guy. I like my food dull and bland, but sometimes you gotta put on a little glitz. A lot of eBay sellers have revitalized their business by giving them a facelift.

Pay attention when you're shopping or researching items on eBay. Fancy listing pages and glitzy store fronts catch your eye. Done properly, they instill confidence in the seller and make you think they're successful and trustworthy.

You can find web designers on eBay, Elance, and Fiverr to help you with this project. Prices can run from as little as five dollars to as much as five or ten thousand dollars, but the payoffs are large if you find the right design.

Start slow if you need to.

Have a custom logo and listing header designed for your eBay store. As time goes on, add a custom listing template, and then a fancy store front.

If you can't afford the expense right now use eBay's store design tools to add a search bar to your store header. Set-up custom categories and subcategories for your eBay store. This makes it easier for shoppers to locate items within your store. Add a couple of promotion boxes to your storefront. Use one to collect email addresses, and another to promote sale items, or shipping specials.

As soon as you're able, put a plan together so you can build a great looking eBay store.

12. Check out eBay's app store

eBay has some great apps available to make running your business smoother. Take a few moments every now and then to page through them. Maybe even try a few of them out.

Here are a few apps I recommend.

- **GoDaddy Bookkeeping** makes it easy to track sales and profits so you know how well your business is doing at any point. GoDaddy Bookkeeping automatically imports sales and purchase information from eBay and PayPal. It lets you connect bank accounts and credit cards you use in your business, and if you sell on eBay, Amazon, and other ecommerce platforms it lets you collect sales data from all of them in one spot. The cost is $9.99 a month, but it's definitely worth it.

- **Endicia Int'l. Advisor** helps you keep track of international shipping rates and requirements. For sellers who ship internationally without using the Global Shipping Program Endicia can help you get rates right. You can also use the full version of Endicia to fulfill all of your domestic and international shipping needs. Costs start at $9.99 per month.

- **Smart Social** is an app that helps you target your eBay listings to followers on Facebook and Twitter. Smart Social lets sellers send listings out one at a time or in batches of 25. You can also set up smart rules to govern how your listings are shared. It's a free app so give it a whirl and see how social media can help grow your sales.

- **My Store Maps** displays locations you have previously shipped packages to. The concept sounds a little cheesy, but many sellers swear by it. Using the app is free.

- **WWW Domain 4 My Store** lets sellers set up a custom domain for your eBay store. Sellers can do it themselves, but it takes some technical know how about domain forwarding to get it right. When you use this app all of the heavy lifting is done for you. Cost is $17.95 per year.

eBay 30 Day Challenge

How to Make $1000 in your First 30 Days
Ready – Set – Sell

eBay
30 DAY
CHALLENGE
How to Make $1000 in Your First
30 Days. Ready. Set. Sell
Shop

Why You Need to Read This Book

Welcome to the *eBay 30 Day Challenge*. The goal of this book is to help you move from zero to $1000 in just 30 days by selling everyday items on eBay.

And, the great thing is—anybody can do it!

Selling on eBay doesn't require any special skills, education, or experience. All you need is access to a computer, a digital camera, and something to sell.

The way this book is laid out, I'm going to tell you a little bit about me—and how I got started selling on eBay. Then we'll talk about eBay, and why it's the best choice for anyone to make money—NOW!

After that, I'll drop a few hints about what sells best on eBay, and how to find these items around your house, at local garage and estate sales, or even at retail stores like Wal-Mart, SAMs, and Costco.

Finally, I'll share everything you need to know to post your first listings on eBay. After that, it's a simple matter of getting started. I'll show you how to post your items, sell—ship—repeat.

That's really all there is to it. Find an item to sell. Determine the best price, and method to list it on eBay. Wait for it to sell. Collect your money, and repeat the process.

About me

I've been selling on eBay for over ten years now.

My typical work week is forty to fifty hours, Monday through Saturday, and maybe another hour on Sunday checking everything and answering emails. Most weeks I make $1000 to $1200. Some weeks I make double that. It just depends on what items I have listed for sale that week.

My schedule goes something like this. I visit garage sales, estate sales, and auctions on Thursday, Friday, and Saturday. Saturday afternoon I clean everything up real good, and get it ready to photograph. Monday, Tuesday, and Wednesday I photograph and list my items.

I mail items daily Monday through Friday to meet eBay's Top Rated Seller requirements.

I've got the eBay app on my cell phone. It's set to send out notifications whenever I receive a question or sell something so I can run my business on the go. If I'm on the line about buying something—I check what it's selling for on eBay or Amazon, and make a buying decision based on real numbers—not some price I hope to get for it.

I know other sellers who hit the road for several weeks at a time like the American Pickers. They check out every estate sale and auction within a hundred miles, or five hundred miles. Most of the people who do this have a partner back home who does the actual listing, packaging, and shipping.

Several of the couples I know who do this are pulling down over $100,000 a year selling on eBay and Amazon. It's just a matter of scaling up once you get the process down.

Keep in mind—the premise behind this book is to get you started, familiarize you with the process, and to help you make your first thousand dollars.

After that, you'll have a good idea if selling on eBay is right for you. My recommendation is to take it slow. Make your first thousand dollars, sit back, and think about what you want from selling on eBay.

Do you want to make a few hundred dollars a month to help make ends meet? Do you need to pay off some bills, save up for a down payment on a new house? Or are you trying to replace your day job, and become a full time at home worker?

No matter which option you choose—it's all possible selling on eBay.

Success is just a matter of getting started.

Why eBay

If you're not familiar with eBay, the best way to think of it is like a ginormous garage sale or yard sale— only it's online.

Buyers and sellers meet on eBay to exchange items and services for cash. In its early days eBay was a perfect marketplace. Most items sold at auction. Whoever made the highest bid won the item. Today all of that has changed, and most items sell with a fixed price. When you see something you like, you click on it, and agree to buy the item at the set price.

At the end of 2013 eBay had nearly 149 million registered users, who spent over $78 billion dollars (exclusive of eBay Motors). Amazon came in just behind eBay with $74 billion dollars in sales, collected from over 243 million registered users. The only larger online marketplace is China's Alibaba and Alibaba Express.

The final fact to keep in mind is the online market place is going mobile. In 2013 just under 30 percent of online sales were completed using mobile devices such as an iPhone, Smart Phone, or tablet. By the end of 2014 that number is expected to approach 50 percent.

The reason I mention this is to help you understand two key factors.

1. Online sales are going up, and

2. More sales are taking place on mobile devices, which means people are shopping on the go—when they're at work, at school, or visiting with friends.

3. To be successful selling on eBay, you need to keep these two trends in mind when you're buying, selling, and listing items. You need the right product, lots of pictures, and a short action filled description.

To make as many sales as possible you need to make it easy for customers to buy from you.

eBay has two different types of listings that will be used by most sellers.

- Auction listings are just like going to a local auction. Items are offered for sale, and the buyer who makes the highest bid wins. Until a few years ago most listings on eBay were sold at auction. Today most items sell at a fixed price.

eBay has a buy-it-now option sellers can add to auction listings. Buy-it-now gives bidders the option to pay a higher price and purchase the item right now, rather than waiting for the auction to close. The main thing to remember is: eBay requires the buy-it-now price to be at least 30 percent higher than the starting price.

Auctions can run for one, three, five, seven, or ten days. The standard auction is for seven days. eBay charges sellers an extra fee if they choose to run a ten day auction.

In most cases, a seven day auction will work just fine to bring the most money for your items. One, three, and five day auctions can be used when you have multiples of fast selling items. An example would be new or used iPhones. Most bidding takes place the last day of an auction so sellers can speed up the process by running shorter term listings.

If you have an expensive item, like a rare book or comic book, that is expected to draw lots of bidders, a ten day auction will attract the maximum number of bidders. As a result you should be able to get a higher price for your item.

- Fixed Price listings are just like going to your local department store. If you see an item you like, you place it in your shopping cart, and buy it at the shelf price. The majority of items sold on eBay today sell at a fixed price.

eBay has a best offer option sellers can use with fixed price listings. It lets buyers send sellers an offer to purchase their item at a discounted price. Buyers are allowed to make three offers, so you can dicker back and forth—and agree on a price that works for both of you.

You can set the length of a fixed price listing, but the two most popular choices are 30 days, and good until cancelled. I recommend the 30 day option because when your item ends you can revisit it to make any necessary changes to give it a better shot at selling the next time around.

What Should I Sell?

What should I sell on eBay?

That's the million dollar question.

The truth is: just about anything will sell on eBay. It's just that some items take longer to sell than others. Examples of fast selling items are electronics, cell phones, name brand clothing, and new release movies and CD's.

A lot of sellers list old books, VHS tapes, sports cards, and other collectibles, but items like these take longer to sell. You have to wait for the right buyer to come along. Sometimes it can take a week; sometimes it can take a year. You've just got to price your items higher to cover the extra time period and listing fees.

eBay Best Sellers

As a general rule the following items are traditionally some of the hottest selling items on eBay.

- Cell phones
- Personal electronics
- Laptops
- Tablets
- Stamps
- Coins
- Rare books
- Name brand clothing

- Designer clothing
- Jewelry
- Watches
- Movies
- Auto Parts
- Non-working electronics (cell phones, tablets, laptops, Kindles)

Some items are a tough sell right now. Here are several items on the slow moving list.

- Damaged or broken items
- Beanie babies
- Newer toys (from the last ten or fifteen years)
- New books
- Dollar store items
- Sports cards (produced after 1980)

I recommend getting started by selling items you already have around the house. That way you can take eBay out for a free trial run and make sure it's right for you.

Not everyone is cut out for online selling.

Contrary to what most magazine articles and how-to books have to say, selling on eBay isn't all sitting around the house in your jammies or undies. There's some actual work involved.

Sourcing Items to Sell

One of the toughest things for new or existing sellers is deciding what to sell on eBay.

My suggestion is to start out selling items you already have around the house. Here's a quick list to get you started.

- Clothes
- DVDs & CDs
- Old electronics (laptops, Kindles, tablets, and cell phones)
- Video games
- Shoes
- Books
- Collectibles (Baseball cards, comic books, Hummel figurines)
- Old landline phones

The list goes on, but you get the idea. Just because you no longer use an item doesn't mean it doesn't have any value. Used clothing and electronics are huge sellers on eBay. Just because your kids stopped playing their old video games doesn't mean someone else won't want them. The same goes for DVDs and CDs. You may be tired of watching and listening to them, but someone else out there is dying for the opportunity.

Not every item will sell. Not right away anyway, but don't be afraid to list them. It is good practice, and many of the items you put up for sale will sell.

It's like paid on the job training.

Yard Sales / Estate Sales / Auctions

The next step for most sellers is to pick up items at yard sales, estate sales, and auctions.

You read about all of these great finds where people pick up rare first edition books for $5.00, or snatch a rare print or painting for a few bucks; all I can say is don't get your hopes up quite that high.

I look for books and magazines I can pick up for a dollar or two and resell for ten or twenty dollars each. Clothes are a good find especially, name brand kids clothing like Gymboree and Osh Kosh. Women's plus size clothing is a consistent seller. Name brand jeans sell well, as do any name brand outfits like Anne Taylor, Banana Republic, Tory Burch, Ralph Lauren, and J Crew.

Collectibles are a crap shoot. Keep your first few buys in the five and ten dollar range. After you get a feel for things raise your limit to twenty-five or fifty dollars. If you get the urge to buy something expensive, check the eBay app on your cell phone first to make sure of what it's selling for. I remember my first few estate sale buys. I picked up some liquor decanters I was sure I could triple my money on. I soon discovered they were selling for less than I paid for them.

Smaller auctions are another great place to pick up items to resell on eBay. I check the listings online or in the paper before I go to make sure they have items that interest me. When I get to the auction site I make a quick round of those items, and check the value on my eBay app. Before the bidding starts I set a limit on how much I'll bid. That way I don't get caught up in the moment and overspend.

Most estate sales run Thursday thru Saturday. Prices are higher the first two days, and are often times reduced by as much as fifty percent on the last day. I normally make two trips. I try to get there early the first day and pick up any items I really want then. I make a note of items I'd like to have and check back the last day of the sale to see if they still have the item, and how much it's selling for. Sometimes you lose the item by waiting, but you don't make anything if you overpay, so you've got to learn to balance time and money.

Retail Stores – Wal-Mart Target T J Maxx

Sometimes the best deals are right under your nose.

Retail stores are constantly changing their inventory—culling out slow sellers, making room for next season's merchandise, or the next holiday. Many eBay sellers have discovered this is a great way to play the system and make a great profit.

Smart sellers hit the clearance aisles every day. Many of them scan bar codes or punch items into their cell phones to determine what the items are selling for on eBay.

Look for clothing that is being closed out at the end of the season. Often times you can find coats, swim suits, and other apparel being closed out for pennies on the dollar. Some sellers resell them immediately, but smart sellers pack the items away until the beginning of the season next year. Often times they can sell the items for full price.

Holiday items are another favorite buy for clearance sellers. You can get some great deals a few days after Christmas, Halloween, and Easter. Once again, you'll make the most money by holding the items until the next year.

I've picked up a lot of close out shoes at Shoe Carnival for ten and fifteen dollars and resold them for twenty-five dollars or more.

If you live in an area with a winning sports team, especially a local college bowl winner you may be able to make a profit purchasing items at full price.

Tools are always a quick sell, as are auto parts, hardware, and small appliances.

Best advice I can give you, if you're new to shopping clearance aisles for resale keep your purchases small. If you're looking at big dollar items check them against the eBay app first, or have someone home at the computer and have them look the item up for you.

The last thing you want to do is lose money.

Posting Your First Listing to eBay

There are six steps to creating a good product listing on eBay.

1. Product research
2. Title
3. Photos
4. Description
5. Price
6. Shipping / Follow up

1. Product Research

The first step to a successful listing is performing product research.

Most times good product research will give you the answers to the other five listing essentials.

To research an item you want to use eBay's advanced search feature. To access it move your cursor to the search box at the top of the eBay page. Just to the right of it you'll see the word *advanced*. Select it. This will take you to the advanced search tool.

The most important thing to remember is: only sold items count. There are a lot of items listed on eBay and Amazon with all sorts of crazy prices, but the only items that count are the ones somebody is willing to pay money for. If nobody laid down any cold hard cash for it, it's just somebody wishing to make a sale. The information in these listings won't help you become a better seller. The only reliable information you can find is in sold listings.

Using the Advanced Search Tool

To get started using the advanced search tool, enter three or four keywords into the search box. In the next section titled *search including* place a check mark by *sold listings*. There are a lot of other options to choose from but for now I would stick with these two, and possibly *buying formats* and *condition*.

The items returned in search will have the price listed in green, and there will be a green bar along the bottom of the listing picture with the word sold written in it.

The first thing you'll notice is the price each item sold for. When you click into an item you'll be able to examine it closer. Make a note of which keywords the seller included in the title, how they worded their description, which buying format they used to list the item, what the starting price was, and if a buy-it-now price was used, make a note of what it was.

Finally, take a look at the pictures. How many pictures did the seller include in their listings? What type of pictures were they—Close-up? Wide angle? Well lit? Were the pictures of just the item being sold, or did they include accessories, too?

2. Title

Think of the title as the entry point to your listing. It should contain all of the search words buyers will use to find your item.

Some sellers like to get cutesy with their titles or write complete sentences, but that's a waste of valuable real estate. eBay gives you 88 characters to describe your item. Make every one of them count. Here are a few items you should include: product name, maker / manufacturer, model number, color, size, condition, warranty, and any common misspellings.

Don't waste words saying awesome, cool, LQQk, or anything like that. No one searches on these terms. Also, resist the urge to capitalize everything. ALL CAPS make your title hard to read, and it makes you look desperate— it's sort of like you're begging for attention.

Final piece of advice: use every character available to you.

3. Photos

Other than your title, good photos are the key to making more sales. Many sellers don't even bother to include a description, they just post a half dozen or a dozen high resolution pictures and invite sellers to decide for themselves if it's the right item for them.

My thought is you want to include as many pictures as possible. Include views from as many different angles as you can. Make sure you snap a few pictures of the packaging and any accessories.

Shoot a quick video of the item you want to sell. It doesn't have to be anything elaborate. If you're selling clothes it could be someone wearing the outfit you're selling. If you're selling toys, show some kids playing with them.

People are fascinated with video. Many times they'll click on it just because it's there. Video is a great way to get extra eyes on your listings.

The first picture you post is the most important. It's the gallery picture for your listing, or the one buyer's will see along with your title in search.

It's the money shot.

You need to make your gallery picture sizzle. It can be a shot of the item and accessories, a close-up of any detail work, or a shot of the product in use. Keep in mind, you can't superimpose words over your gallery image, and it can't be a drawing. It's got to be a picture.

eBay has a few other rules and requirements for pictures. All pictures are required to be a minimum of 500 pixels along the longest side. eBay recommends 1600 pixels for the best viewing experience. The reason this is important is when buyers click on your images to blow them up, the larger your picture, the more detail they're going to be able to see.

Let's say you're selling a hand tooled leather saddle. You can talk forever about horses, cattle, and cowboys riding on the open plains, but one close up picture will close the deal quicker. When the buyer clicks on a picture they can zoom in section by section to really check out all of the detailed leather work. It's the next best thing to being there.

The same thing goes when an item you're selling is damaged. You can describe the damage, or you can show the damage and invite buyers to decide for themselves how bad it is.

Good pictures will help you make more sales. Good pictures will help to prevent returns and misunderstandings. Invest in a good camera, and take time out to learn how to use it. Your investment will pay off in increased sales.

4. Description

A good description should tell the buyer everything they need to know to make them want to buy your item. At the same time, it should be short, concise, and have plenty of white space.

Buyers read item descriptions the same way they read blog posts and other internet content. They scan your listings looking for details that interest them.

Make it easy for buyers to find the information they need to know. Give your item details in short bursts. Use a large headline followed by one or two short sentences. Use another headline, and include all of the specs or other pertinent details using a bulleted list.

Reader's eyes are naturally drawn to bold text, and we're used to finding the info we're looking for in bullet points, so our eyes go there next.

Here's an example of what you should shoot for.

1955 Topps Willie Mays Sports Card

If you're a fan of 1955 Topps baseball cards you know the Willie Mays card is one of the most desirable. Take it from me—this is one of the best examples of that card you'll find.

Item Details

- 1955 Topps Baseball card
- Card # 194
- 4 solid corners
- Mint to near mint condition
- Perfectly centered back
- Lustrous vibrant color – just like the day it was printed
- Send this card in for grading and watch the value go up.

One other thing you will notice is I made a call to action at the end of the description—"Send this card in for grading and watch the value go up." Another effective call to action would be, "Grab this key Willie Mays card now before another collector outbids you."

A call to action doesn't always work, but it gives you one last shot at making the sale.

Keep it short, simple, and to the point.

Buyers don't want to waste time wading through a lot of clutter and unnecessary words. They want to find the information they want—NOW! Help them find it, and you will make more sales.

One other thing. Never—ever fill your descriptions with conditions, policies, disclaimers, and other gobbledygook. Nothing turns buyers off quicker than looking at this stuff.

Keep your descriptions positive. Don't tell buyers what you won't do. Tell them what you will do. Focus on helping customers buy from you. Don't warn them that they need to follow through with their bid, and that their bid's a valid legal contract and all that other nonsense. All of that stuff only does one thing—It tells potential buyers you're a prick, and they should move on to the next listing.

5. Price

Setting the price is part art, part science, and a whole lot of luck.

Some sellers swear by starting every auction at 99 cents and letting the market set the price. Other sellers shoot for the moon. They slap a crazy price on every item they sell, and add a best offer to see what buyers are thinking. Some sellers shoot to double or triple their initial investment and price everything accordingly.

There's no one set way to price your items.

My suggestion is to research everything. Before you list anything on eBay run an advanced search by sold items so you know what your item recently sold for. Most often, you'll discover it sold for a range of prices depending upon condition and how well the description was written.

If you're selling your item in an auction listing, set your starting price at the lowest price the item sold for, and then set a buy it now price just above the highest selling price. This virtually assures that your item will sell.

If you're selling your item in a fixed price listing set the selling price just above the highest price the item most recently sold for. Include a buy-it-now, and set it to automatically accept at the lowest recent selling price, or another price that is acceptable to you.

If you have an item that hasn't sold recently or is totally new to eBay you have a few choices.

If you have a suggested selling price in mind—list the item as fixed price, and add a best offer. This will help you see where the market is at.

Alternatively, you could start your item at 99 cents, $9.99, or some other price, and see where the market takes it. After you've sold one or two items, you can use this pricing information to price your other listings.

6. Shipping / follow up

The first decision you have to make is whether to offer free shipping or charge for shipping.

eBay encourages sellers to offer free shipping, and usually ranks items with free shipping higher in search, so if your margins allow you to offer free shipping, do it.

If free shipping isn't an option for what you're selling, check what other sellers are charging for shipping on similar items. There are several different options for showing shipping charges. If you can, wrap part of the shipping fees into your item price, and charge less shipping than other sellers. If you can't do that, try to charge $1.00 less for shipping than your competitors.

eBay offers several different shipping options.

- **Flat rate**. Flat rate shipping means you charge the same shipping fees to all customers no matter where they are located. The advantage is buyers know exactly what they have to pay.

- **Calculated shipping**. Calculated shipping uses eBay's shipping calculator to determine shipping fees based upon where your buyer lives. The advantage is buyers who live closer to you get a break on shipping, which can reduce their total purchase price.

- **Freight**. Freight shipping is for larger items that need to ship by motor truck. The eBay shipping calculator only works up to 150 pounds, so if your item weighs more than that you need to use flat rate.

- **Local pickup**. Local pickup lets buyers pickup items at your home or business location. Be cautious if you accept payment through PayPal. With local pickup you don't have delivery confirmation if the buyer opens an item not received case against you.

Follow up

Check your email at least two or three times a day when you have items for sale.

The quicker you can respond to buyers the more likely you are to close the sale. When you respond to a customer be sure to answer their question completely. Also, take a few minutes to talk up the item you are selling. Say something like, "Thank you for inquiring about the widget I have for sale on eBay. It's a great widget, and in fantastic shape. You can read a little bit more about it in this blog post."

It only takes a few more minutes when you respond to your buyer, but it helps to build confidence in your eBay store and what you're selling.

If you receive a complaint after you sell an item, don't panic. Thank the customer for contacting you, and tell them you understand their concerns. Most often you can save the sale by taking a few moments to explain how to use the item, or by answering any other questions your buyer may have.

If the customer insists on returning your item, accept the return graciously, and outline your return policies. If the buyer is required to pay return shipping let them know, and tell them how soon they can expect a refund.

If the return is because of a defect in the item or a misstatement in the listing—apologize for the mistake. Offer a refund, or replacement if available, and once again explain the return process.

Handling inquiries and returns professionally will help ensure positive feedback from the transaction.

Tips & Tricks to Increase Your Sales

1. **Use eBay & PayPal shipping tools**. When you print your labels using the eBay shipping tool it automatically transfers buyer information into the shipping label saving you time. It also transfers tracking information back into the item listing page so buyers can track their items progress. The other advantage is you pay for shipping as you go. Each time you print a label the shipping price is deducted from your PayPal account.

2. **Get free shipping supplies from the USPS**. Stop paying for boxes, and packing supplies. The post office will give you free boxes and envelopes for items you ship by priority and express mail.

3. **Use GoDaddy Bookkeeping to track your income and expenses**. eBay has an app called GoDaddy Bookkeeping that can help you keep track of your earnings and expenses. The great thing is it can automatically import information from eBay and PayPal, as well as from any credit cards and bank accounts you connect to the app. If you sell on Amazon or Etsy, GoDaddy Bookkeeping works with them, too. The cost is $9.99 per month.

4. **Add YouTube videos to your auction listings.**
Videos can help engage auction viewers, and
increase the likelihood they will buy from you. It's
simple to add YouTube videos to your listing
descriptions. Just upload your video to YouTube,
and select use *old embed code*. Paste the code into
your item description where you want the video to
appear.

5. **Use Templates or Sell Similar item to streamline
your listings**. When you use a template or the sell
similar item option all of your listing information is
transferred to the new listing. This saves you from
typing repetitive information.

6. **Offer Shipping discounts**. When you offer shipping
discounts, customers are likely to purchase
additional items from you. eBay gives you several
options to choose from. You can ship additional
items for free, or at a reduced rate.

7. **Skip listing upgrades**. Whenever you list an item
eBay offers several listing upgrades that are
supposed to increase visibility for your item. Most
of them are a waste of money. The only one that
may help is subtitle. Depending upon the item you
are selling, subtitle can give buyers the extra nudge
they need to click into your auction and give it a
look.

8. **Opt into eBay's Global Shipping Program**. eBay's Global Shipping program lets you sell internationally without all of the hassle of filling out customs forms and such. To get started you just need to select the Global Shipping Program option. If your item sells internationally, you ship it to eBay's shipping center in the United States and you're done.

9. **Only accept PayPal**. eBay gives sellers a number of payment options, but 99 percent of buyers use PayPal. Don't waste time fooling around with other payment providers.

10. **Always ship with a tracking number**. Ship all of your items with a tracking number. It keeps everyone involved in the transaction honest. Tracking allows buyers to know where their package is any step along the way. If something goes wrong, it can protect you if an item not received case is filed. If you ship with eBay's shipping tool, tracking is automatically uploaded into the item listing.

11. **Include best offer in your fixed price listings**. Best offer lets sellers send you an offer for items you list by fixed price. Each time they send you an offer, you have the chance to accept it, or send a counter offer. Buyers are able to send three best offers on

each item. Don't be afraid to bargain back and forth if the offer you receive is too low.

12. **Include buy-it-now in your auction listings**. Buy-it-now is an option where buyers can buy your auction listing for a set price, and end the auction immediately. In my experience, one in nine auctions will end with a buy-it-now. The only requirement is your buy-it-now price must be at least thirty percent higher than your starting price.

13. **Accept returns**. Most people are reluctant to buy an item sight unseen from a buyer they don't know. You can overcome this fear and sell more items by offering to accept returns. In my experience, less than one in five hundred items is returned, so it shouldn't be a major concern.

14. **Schedule Pickups with the USPS**. Stop going to the post office. If you are shipping at least one item by priority or express mail you can schedule a pickup, and the post office will come to your house and pick up your packages.

15. **Open an eBay store**. If you sell a lot of items on eBay, an eBay store can help you ramp up sales even more. eBay stores allow you to collect all of your items in one spot on eBay. If you choose to, you can brand your store and listings so they are easily recognizable as your own. An eBay store also

opens up several other features including being able to build an email list and send newsletters to your subscribers, and to use Mark Down Manager—an eBay tool that lets you discount items in your store for a short period of time.

eBay fees

On eBay sellers have to pay to play. eBay charges a myriad of fees. These include listing fees, final value fees, upgrade fees, and store fees (if you have a store).

The following list is included to give you an idea of eBay fees. It is up to date as of August 25th, 2014.

Seller fees are based upon whether you have an eBay store or not, and the level of eBay store you have.

- Sellers without an eBay store receive fifty free auction listings each month. Final value fees average ten percent of the selling price.
- Sellers with a Basic eBay store pay $15.99 per month. They receive 150 free auction or fixed price listings each month. Final value fees average ten percent of the selling price.
- Sellers with a Premium eBay store pay $59.99 per month. They receive 500 free auction or fixed price listings each month. Final value fees average ten percent of the selling price.
- Sellers with an eBay Anchor store pay $199.99 per month. They receive 2500 free auction or fixed price listings. Final value fees average ten percent of the selling price.

Sellers who subscribe to an eBay store for a one year period can receive additional discounts. Top Rated

Sellers who meet certain requirements also qualify for a twenty percent discount on final value fees.

Final Wrap up

Selling on eBay isn't rocket science. Most of it comes down to common sense. Find popular products that people like and enjoy. Offer them at a great price, and treat your customers fairly.

When you're first getting started, sell items you have around the house. It will give you practice listing and monitoring listings. It's also a great way to put a few extra bucks in your pocket, and decide if selling on eBay is right for you.

Pick up your first items to resell at local yard sales, estate sales, and auctions. You can also find some great bargains shopping the clearance aisles at retail stores like Wal-Mart, Target, and T J Maxx. If you live near an outlet mall you should be able to find plenty of items to resell there.

When you list your items keep the six steps to a great listing in mind.

1. **Product research**. Research everything. Look for keywords, description ideas, and pricing info used in listings that closed successfully.
2. **Title**. You have 88 characters to tell the world what you've got. Make every one of them count. Include: maker, model number, color, size, condition, warranty, free shipping, and other relevant info.

3. **Photos**. Use plenty of photos taken from a number of different angles. Make sure your photos are at least 500 pixels on the longest edge, eBay recommends 1600 pixels.
4. **Description**. Keep your description short and to the pint. Use headlines, short sentences, and bullet points. White space is your friend.
5. **Price**. Use the advanced search tool to determine the appropriate starting price for every item you sell. Use a variety of fixed price and auction listings to drive buyers to your other listings or your eBay store.
6. **Shipping / follow up**. Ship your items within the handling period you set, and be sure to include tracking on all items. Use the eBay or PayPal shipping tool to make shipping your items easier. Answer all questions as quickly as possible, and give buyers more info than they asked for.

That's all there is to it.

Good luck and great selling. The **eBay 30 Day Challenge** will help you reach your goals quickly.

Other Books by Braun Schweiger

eBay 30 Day Challenge: How to Make $1000 in Your First 30 Days Ready – Set – Sell

eBay Selling Made Easy

Banging Your Way Across Craigslist: How to Pick Up, Flirt, Seduce, and Sleep With Women on Craigslist